Anyone Can Speak 7 Languages!

HIPPO FAMILY CLUB

This book was originally published as a collection of articles in the Sankei Newspaper (September 9, 1997 through October 18, 1997) entitled, "Opening Up the Multilingual World - The Mystery of Babies and Language," which has been revised and given new titles.

Published by:
Lex Institute / Hippo Family Club, Ace-Shoto Bldg., 1-4-7 Shoto, Shibuya-ku, Tokyo 150 Japan
TEL:03-3467-6151

US Office
LEX America, 68 Leonard Street, Belmont, MA 02178
TEL:617-489-5800
E-mail HIPPO@lexlrf.com

© Lex Institute / Hippo Family Club 1997

First Published 1997

ISBN 4-906519-05-9

All rights reserved. No part of this book may be reproduced or transmitted in any from or by any means, electronic or mechanical, including photocopying, recording, or by any information storage and retrieval system, without permission in writing from the Publisher. The publisher has made every effort to trace the ownership of all copyrighted material and to secure the necessary permissions. In the event of any question arising as to the use of any material, the Publisher, while expressing every regret for any inadvertent error, will be happy to make any necessary corrections.

Printed in Japan

Foreword

Anyone, by the age of 3 or 4 will easily be able to speak the language spoken around them. If they are in an environment in which there are 3 or 4 languages being spoken constantly, they will grow up to speak those languages. This is what defines us as being human. Take for example the case of 5 and 6 year old Taro and Hanako who come to New York when their father is transferred by his company. Within six months to a year, they acquire perfect English just playing in the park with their friends. The same is true for adults too, especially adults from multilingual parts of the world such as India or Africa, where hundreds of languages coexist. Less than one year after arriving in Japan, they are able to speak Japanese proficiently and very naturally.

How does this happen?

They would probably answer the question like this,

"In no time at all, without even realizing it."

We call this natural process the "natural acquisition of languages." But we have not really given much thought to what is so "natural" about it. What is nature doing?

Searching for the answer to this question and discovering a language to describe it is the goal of Natural Science. There is however one condition which must be followed strictly when investigating natural phenomena. We must observe only those events which occur repeatedly. Behind them, we will find simply defined rules. This is the firm belief of natural scientists.

Since the birth of mankind, humans have developed language, which continues to evolve as we use it.

If humans were mammals that did not need language to survive, we would never have created it. Nature has no place for unnecessary toys. Humans cannot survive in isolation. We live by creating a language network and using that network to find resonance with other humans. Language is the necessary result of this process.

One summer, a pigeon appeared on our balcony and began building a nest. Two weeks after it had laid its egg, a chick was born. Within a matter of weeks it had grown up to be a mirror image of its mother. One morning, a little while after we noticed it had begun to practice flying, it perched upon the railing with its mother. The next moment, it took to the air and flew off into its new world. It happened so quickly, it was like watching a film which has been speeded up. I was impressed down to the bottom of my heart.

Then it suddenly occurred to me, this is a language too!

From the time the first cell of the egg was produced, it contained all the components necessary for it to become a pigeon. By the time it hatched, it had multiplied into trillions of cells but the cells still expressed the whole form of the pigeon at that moment in time. All living things express themselves completely as a whole at every moment along the way to adulthood.

A mother plays with her child of 2 or 3 months. The baby is in the best of spirits as can be determined by its unceasing cries of "ah—ah" and "oh—oh" Without ever getting bored, the mother happily replies to these sounds. She proudly tells her friends,
"My baby is talking quite a bit these days."

Already, their language world is complete. Like the multiplying cells of a living organism, language is always complete and whole at each moment in time.

Until now, language had been examined only from the outside as an "object" and analyzed according to a certain set of rules. Language education developed along these same lines, gathering the parts — pronunciation, words and grammar — together to build a language program. However, researchers had failed to view the natural phenomenon of language acquisition in its entirety.

For example, by the time they are 3 or 4, children generally do not make major grammatical errors. Why is this? To use an analogy, let's say grammar is like the nervous system of a living creature. The nervous system will develop in unison with the creature as it heads toward adulthood. If languages are not taken into account in their entirety, it stands to reason that we will have to depend on an artificial means to acquire them.

Let's search for the naturalness of language.

"Let's learn from babies." That's our motto. But no matter how hard we look from the outside, it is impossible to produce a true image of what happens inside a baby.

Finally, impatience led someone to say, "Then let's become a baby."

This was the beginning of the Hippo Family Club's multilingual activities 16 years ago. From there, we began to search for the "baby" which still lies within all of us. We tried to create an environment in which we could "master" new languages using only our ears, mouths and our hearts (in people-to-people connections).

For adults, becoming a "baby" was easier said than done. We made one mistake after another. Progress was slow, but sure, as we swung back and forth between the "natural" baby stage and the "unnatural" adult stage. As each person tried to act "like a baby" we began to share some of the same experiences. We found the balance in nature.

Adults who began to master a number of languages "in no time at all, without even knowing it" said,

"Oh I see, that's why babies can do it!"

Everyone made the same discovery as they encountered "the baby within".

The 27 chapters in this book were written by seven HIPPO Family Club members. These members, many of them parents, share their experiences and their inner discoveries. To us, it is a monumental chronicle describing the natural phenomenon of language from within ourselves.

How are living things organized and how do they evolve? We have come to see the development of language as a mirror image of this phenomenon.

Babies discover their world through language, and thus discover more and more about themselves, but they are not alone. Adults are also following the same path. On a HIPPO Family Club journey, anyone can discover a more beautiful self through language exploration.

December 1997

Contents

Foreword	3
Adults and Babies Begin a Multilingual Adventure Together	8
Leap Over Language Barriers	10
Familiar Sounds Resonate	12
Emotion-filled Experiences Bring Languages Closer	14
Language is a Gift for All Ages	16
Languages are Like Music: Begin by Humming the Tune	18
Scenes Bring Meaning to Sounds	20
Jump into the "Sea of Language"	22
Play with the Sounds and Meaning will Follow	24
Follow the Natural Path and You Can't Make a Mistake	26
Language Acquired Unconsciously	28
Language Develops in an Open Mind	30
Baby-Talk is Adults' First Step Too!	32
First Come Sounds - then Letters	34
A Lifetime of Growth from a Single Homestay	36
A Kinder, Gentler Self	38

I Didn't Know I Spoke French!	40
Each Language Has a Unique Melody	42
Adults are Prodigies Too!	44
No Classes, No Teachers, No Test!	46
Stop Worrying and Just Speak!	48
A Bigger World with New Friends	50
Mathematics is a Language	52
Natural Science: Researching the Obvious	54
Ears, Mouth and Heart are Open to any Language	56
There's No Such Thing as a "Foreign" Language at HIPPO	58
Search for the Baby Within	60

Illustrations by Mirei Sakakibara
Layout by Ryuji Fujieda, Akiko Kuramochi
Title and Catch Copy by Takayuki Arakawa

Adults and Babies Begin a Multilingual Adventure Together

One day while I was on the way home from work a yellow poster announcing a symposium caught my eye. The title read, "Let's Speak in 7 Languages!" "Just English is hard enough for a Japanese-speaker, but 7 languages? That's impossible," I thought. "Still it would be really amazing to be able to speak 7 languages." Unconsciously my fingers reached for the attached flyer, and I turned my feet in the direction of the symposium.

There, topics such as "Absorbing language like a baby..." and "Anyone, even adults, can acquire many languages at once" were discussed, using concrete real life examples in a way that was easy to understand and convincing. "It's true, given three years, a baby will always be able to speak." My eyes were opened to the mystery of something I had always taken for granted. With natural acquisition perhaps even I might be able to speak many languages.

At that time, I happened to be pregnant. After my marriage, my job had remained at the center of my life, but now that I was pregnant I was about to embark on a *new* life with my baby.

"Embracing this opportunity, I will become a 7-language 'baby'. Then I can enjoy the language adventure right from the beginning, together with my baby," I thought. And so I decided to join the HIPPO Family Club.

Several days later I went to my first HIPPO Family Club meeting. It was one surprise after

another. First, adults and children danced and played games together accompanied by music tapes. Businessmen, still in their neckties and wiping away sweat, were completely absorbed. "What good is all of this?" I thought as I watched and began to move my body like everyone else. Logic aside, the 30 or so minutes spent in a return to childhood were a lot of fun.

Next, a story tape began to play. Everyone spoke along with the tape, using gestures at the same time. They all looked like they were having fun. I didn't even know what language it was, but I was in another world, having a great time. At that moment..."It's OK if you don't understand the words," said the person next to me with a smile. "Huh?" My eyes opened wide in amazement. "What's the point of memorizing words you can't understand?" I wondered.

Lastly, we sat in a circle and passed a microphone from person to person. Adults and children, each person in his or her own way, began to speak in different languages. From smooth speakers to new members speaking their first few words of Korean, there were all kinds. After each person finished, everyone praised him or her, "That's great. Good job!" The speakers and listeners all looked happy.

On the one hand, it didn't seem like a way to acquire languages. But, if these activities really led me to speak many languages… My doubts turned to enthusiasm.

Leap Over Language Barriers

By becoming a parent, I made my language world richer in just one stroke. Even before she was born, I began to speak to the baby inside of me, and from the time she was born it was natural to speak to her constantly. The best way to put it is, "The baby pulled words from my mouth, one after the other". My daughter Kanako tried to open her eyes, move her head, and wave her arms and legs. It's the role of the earnest new parent to decipher the baby's messages found in her expressions and small movements.

By the time she was three months old, Kanako would look at the person in front of her and make sounds. "Argh" when she was happy, "an, an" when she was unhappy, and later "mama", "babu", or "apa" and an increasing variety of sounds.

Generally speaking, I was able to understand the meaning of each sound. By now, she already had a rich language. It wasn't at all a one-sided conversation. My conversation times with Kanako were fun and satisfying – our communication was sufficient for both of us.

At that time, the idea came up in my neighborhood for our "Family" (HIPPO Family Club) to host a researcher from Costa Rica. I was feeling negative about it because I couldn't speak any Spanish yet. But my husband, tipsy and in an expansive mood, agreed to take him in.

I was in fact just beginning to listen to the HIPPO Family Club tapes and "Hola" (Hello) was

about the only word of Spanish that I could understand. "Oh no, what'll I do?" I worried. As we exchanged greetings at our first meeting, my nervousness reached it's peak. Unbelievably, he couldn't speak anything but Spanish!

But then I became aware that I had somehow understood him say so, *in Spanish*. I eagerly applied the powers of my imagination to figure out what he was trying to communicate through his puzzled expression, hand gestures, and the sound of his voice. Before we knew it, we adults were becoming like babies.

First of all, I was surprised at how well we could understand each other through expressions and gestures. Moreover, by the end of the short one-night homestay I could generally understand the meaning in the sounds of his voice speaking Spanish, which accompanied his gestures. We were invariably able to understand each other and it was a really fun two days.

As for Kanako, she sat on his lap smiling happily. To her, Spanish and Japanese were all the same. To Kanako's, "ah, ah", he replied with his beaming face and his Spanish.

Through this brief experience, I came to believe that with an open heart and the zest for mutual understanding, it's possible to become friends with people of any country and speakers of any language. I'm confident of it.

Familiar Sounds Resonate

When I joined the HIPPO Family Club, the first thing that happened was a huge box of tapes arrived. I was stunned at the enormous number of tapes, but grabbed the first one which came to hand, and began to listen. HIPPO says, "Play it like background music – it doesn't matter if you understand or not."

At first I didn't even know which language I was hearing. But after two or three months I could distinguish among the different languages. Each language has its own melody and its own rhythm. Therefore, it's not difficult to distinguish among the languages. As when listening to lots of musical pieces over and over, there's no way to mix them up.

As the sounds of the tape showered over me, I didn't understand the meaning, but the sounds which I heard collected inside of me. Then, they gradually began to flow from my mouth. Although I couldn't understand the meaning, I could speak the sounds just like the tape. This became very comfortable for me. At HIPPO, this is called, "Singing the sounds."

Around the time that I had developed the ability to sing almost all of the Spanish tape, my family daringly decided to venture on our first homestay – to Spain. At that stage I thought that greetings and self-introductions were about all the Spanish I could actually speak.

When I said, "Hola," a storm of Spanish came back at me and my mind went completely

blank. But when I calmed down a little, I began to feel some resonance between my host's Spanish and the sounds I had heard on the tape and collected inside of me. Some of the sounds were the same. This was the beginning of my "understanding".

One day, our host family had all gone out leaving my family home alone. Suddenly, the intercom buzzed! Without realizing what I was doing, I pressed the button. Not surprisingly, rapid-fire Spanish came at me through the intercom. Although I couldn't understand each word one by one, the person seemed to be asking if the family was at home.

The answer, "Madre salida. Juan también." (Mother is out. And Juan, too.), promptly jumped from my mouth. I don't really know how I was able to say those words. But when the appropriate situation arose, the sounds, which I had thought were just sounds inside of me, were pulled out of me as language with meaning.

Another time, soon after, our host said, "Mira, caballos!" (Look at the horses!) to my two year-old daughter, Kanako. Reflexively, she began to sing a section from the Spanish tape, "Caballos, corderos, cerdos..." (Horses, sheep, pigs...) Our host and I looked at each other in astonishment!

Through this process, Kanako will eventually be a speaker of many languages.

Emotion-filled Experiences Bring Languages Closer

My daughter Kanako was very late with potty-training. But, among her friends at HIPPO Family Club was a boy who had worn diapers until the age of three. When I looked at him, I thought with relief, "If I don't try too hard to teach her, she'll do it naturally when she's ready."

Language is also something which cannot be taught. It is something which is discovered through interaction with the people around you. Humans have the ability to discover human language. Some may be a little slower or a little faster, but that doesn't matter.

One day while in the *back* seat of the car, Kanako grumbled, "I want to sit in the back." I didn't say, "You mean *front*, not *back*," because that would be less interesting. In any case, before I knew it, she would be able to say it herself.

In the same way, when I went to Spain on my first homestay, I didn't know in Spanish what was up, what was down, what was right, or what was left. But, by the time I left Spain, I was able to say them correctly.

Adults have completely forgotten how they acquired their first language. But, with the multilingual world of HIPPO Family Club I've had the experience of being a "language baby", right from the first step.

Since I knew the joy of discovering even just one word, I was especially able to look forward to Kanako's time of discovery. For me, it wasn't, "She can't talk *yet*," but "In due time,

she'll be able to say *this* and *this*." Because of HIPPO, the joy of raising my daughter has been increased ten-fold or twenty-fold.

Kanako's growing up is layered together with my multilingual experiences. Being an adult, I sometimes lapsed suddenly into the grown-up's, "What does this word mean?" or "Oops, I made a mistake." At those times I realized Kanako was giving me a message to relax and take my time.

In addition, I have had the benefit of my many HIPPO friends who eagerly listened to my musings on these subjects. It might seem like the gushing of a proud parent, but everyone always listened carefully and replied, "wonderful, wonderful!" They have each had the same experience of discovering their own language, so when they said, "wonderful," it came from the heart.

"She sucked her thumb… She held her toy… She laughed out loud… When I called her name, she turned…" I never tire of watching the day by day changes in a baby. At the same time, the baby is saying, "Don't take these things for granted. Be astonished! Be impressed!"

For me too, when I spoke my first word of Korean, "Anyong haseyo" (Hello), my friends praised me, "Excellent!" A part of me felt a little embarrassed, but mostly I was glad. In that moment, I felt the Korean language come closer to me.

Language is
a Gift for All Ages

Previously, it had been more a question of whether or not she could count 1, 2, 3, 4, ... as she sang the theme song to a cartoon show in the bathtub. But, one day my three-year old daughter, Maroka, suddenly said, "I'm gonna do my brother's song!" Then she began to sing the opening paragraph of the HIPPO Family Club tape, "HIPPO Goes Overseas," in Chinese in a clear voice.

"Incredible! When did she pick that up?" I wondered with surprise.

"I can do Junko-chan's, too," my daughter said, and began the Spanish version, "HIPPO cruza los mares." And then my daughter said, "I'll do Kimi-chan's," and sang the English version, and then "Shun-kun's" in fluent-sounding Malay.

Finally, saying, "I'll do Daddy's, too," she gave the Japanese version. I remembered that the other day my husband had mimicked the Japanese tape in a funny voice.

"Wow, that's amazing, you sounded just like Daddy," I exclaimed. On and on, my daughter and I were carried away.

At the HIPPO multilingual gatherings, there's a time when everyone sits together in a circle and shares many languages. Small children join with the adults and, eyes sparkling, they sing and speak their favorite phrases. When my daughter spoke of "My brother's..." or "So-and-so's...," that's what she meant.

Maroka had also sung along at those times and hummed the words, but I was surprised to hear her speak them so clearly. To us adults, those phrases are Chinese or Spanish, but to my daughter the words weren't associated with countries.

Those were the sounds of the tapes we always play at home, and more than that, language belonging to her friends. Different sounds call up the faces of various dear friends - how very joyful!

Maroka can now speak Japanese quite well. To the question, "Why is she able to speak so well?" the answer must be, "She received language as gifts from the people around her."

The same is true for adults. At the time sounds on the French tape were still indistinguishable to me, someone recited a portion of the tape clearly at a HIPPO gathering.

The next day, while I was casually playing the tape at home it happened. As the tape played over that section, that person's face appeared before me. In that part only, the previously indistinguishable French words appeared clearly as she had said them. And, before I knew it, I was able to say them, too.

For adults, as well as children, "Language is something we receive from the people around us."

Languages are Like Music: Begin by Humming the Tune

What happens when we learn new songs?

When we like a song, unconsciously we begin to hum it. At first, we may get just a part of the melody, but when we finally go all the way from beginning to end, that feels good. Even if there is a part where we're unsure of the words, we can get through that part by humming, and still sing the song.

Adults, who have no problem with this when it comes to karaoke, suddenly become strangely defensive when the subject is language study. They feel they have to start with pronunciation practice, memorize vocabulary words one-by-one, and that they better not make any mistakes. This "from the parts to the whole" method is ridiculously difficult.

At HIPPO Family Club we often say, "Sing the sounds." This is more than just a metaphor. At first we try to sing the big wave of language, the rhythm and melody which constitute the "Chinese-ness" of Chinese, or the "French-ness" of French.

Babies love songs. At HIPPO gatherings, even babies who can't walk yet will sway happily to the sounds of a song tape. Slightly bigger kids, age two or three, will sing "London Bridge" or songs from various countries with shining, proud faces. Some kids can sing the song exactly as it is on the tape, while others are just getting the general flow. Even though a child may sing

only the end of each phrase clearly, while humming the rest, the way he catches the characteristic rhythm and melody of the language is worthy of a standing ovation.

When we adults listen to the tapes and imitate the sounds, the same thing happens. For example, when I first heard Korean, I couldn't pick anything out, but as I got used to hearing it, unconsciously I began to hum it like a song, vocalizing the ends of phrases just like babies do, "~~yo, ~~eyo, ~~da, ~~nida."

In this way, still without understanding the meaning, I came to be able to speak all the words, as if in a song. There was no way to make a mistake. Since I didn't even know where the breaks between words were, pieces such as "past tense" or "plural form" or "articles" were all hidden inside of the whole, and it was impossible to be confused by them.

"From the whole to the parts." This is the secret of how babies discover language. Through natural experience we've found that adults are no different from babies.

My husband is very good at doing imitations. Hardly thinking about what language he is hearing on the tape, he is soon able to imitate the tape perfectly. When asked, "Why are you so good at it?" He replies seriously, "It must be because I don't try too hard. And because I'm doing it together with friends and family."

Scenes Bring Meaning to Sounds

When my son, Shohei, was two, our family went to stay in the Mexican countryside on a HIPPO Family Club homestay. Of course, our two weeks in Mexico were fantastic, but after we returned home, interesting things *continued* to happen.

After we got back, I was playing a HIPPO 7-Language Tape (the language changes with each change of scene in the story). When the scene switched to Spanish, my son yelled, "Mama, I hear Elba!" To him, the Spanish on the tape sounded like the voice of his Mexican host mother.

Then, one day two months later, I served cereal for breakfast, which was a rare event in our home.

I was quite startled when, on seeing the cereal, Shohei said automatically, "Poquito." In Mexico, we usually had cereal for breakfast. When Shohei's dish was empty, Elba would say, "¿Quieres más? ¿Poquito?" (Do you want more? A little?) Those words and that scene were linked together in Shohei's mind.

Around the same time, Shohei would often say, "Mama, do 'Chaparrito'," as he nestled up to me. Mexican people particularly cherish small children. When they saw Shohei, people

would run up with open arms, calling, "Chaparrito! Que bonito!" (What a handsome young fellow!)

In Mexico, I didn't have to worry about housekeeping. I could only generally understand the language, so like Shohei, I was relaxed and easygoing. But once we returned to Japan, I became Shohei's stern mother again, always yelling, "Hurry up!... Stop that!" At these times when Shohei said, "Do 'Chaparrito'," he meant "Mama, treasure me, treat me special like the Mexicans did."

As for me, after we came back from Mexico, the Spanish on the tape sounded completely different. "Oh, this is what Elba said *that* time... Ah, this is what my host dad said *then*." As soon as I heard a phrase on the tape, I would remember the scene in Mexico where I had heard it used.

As if black and white sounds were slowly suffused in color, the meaning gradually comes into view. If I try to speak Spanish, I can't speak well. But when the scene comes to me, Spanish flows freely for me.

When I think of Mexico, I always hear Elba's voice saying, "Feliz viaje" (Have a nice trip).

Jump into the "Sea of Language"

I first met Mrs. Lee at a round-table discussion in my son's first-grade class. When I discovered that the woman sitting next to me, Mrs. Lee, was Korean, almost without thinking I said, "Anyong haseyo" (Hello). At this, Mrs. Lee's face just lit up!

"Don't forget the importance of Japan's closest neighbor. We will never discover the world while ignoring Korea," says Yo Sakakibara, founder of the HIPPO Family Club. Fifteen years ago, at Sakakibara's suggestion, Korean language tapes were added to existing English and Spanish tapes, and multilingual activities were born.

The fact that we couldn't read Korean writing was a lucky thing. We had to depend on our ears and mouths only. We listened to the tapes as we never had before. Like babies, we jumped into the new "Sea of Language" and found language in our own way, at our own pace.

Babies don't listen silently. They are always playing with sounds. Since we began Korean fresh, without preconceived expectations, we were able to shape the sounds from the tape easily. Children and adults all worked from the same starting place.

Through our experiences with the Korean language, we began to understand how interesting the multilingual world is. By the time I had made friends in Korea, and could speak Korean

pretty comfortably, I realized I could *read* Korean writing, too.

With English and Spanish, we adults felt comfortable because we could look at the textbook and read the letters. When we had trouble saying anything, our hands would reach for the text. Once we could read the words, we wanted to look them up in a dictionary. And, we started thinking about grammar. Then came the unproductive worry about making mistakes, until finally we were afraid to open our mouths at all.

Letters are not sounds. If you get caught up with letters first, and try to teach yourself the sounds, you will distort them unnaturally. It's because we have the sounds first that we are able to read.

Slipping back and forth between Japanese and Korean without noticing, Mrs. Lee and I became very close friends. As Mrs. Lee remarked, it was particularly nice that our talk wasn't limited to, "How's Korea?" and "How's Japan?" Our talk was made of everyday conversation like, "My husband is always working late," and "The children won't listen to me." And, I was most happy when Mrs. Lee said to me, "When I'm with you I feel just like when I'm with my Korean friends."

Play with the Sounds and Meaning will Follow

We have three sons - eleven months, almost three years-old, and five years-old - in our home. I leave it up to you to imagine what it's like here.

When my youngest son was just over five months old, he began to make frequent humming sounds. The sounds were not a clear "ah" or "wa", but a wavering "ahuhahuah". Always when he found a new sound, he would repeat it over and over, seeming to delight in it. My two older sons found this amusing and would imitate the sounds, turning our home into the temporary abode of monsters.

Now that I think about it, both my eldest and middle sons discovered the same sounds around the same time. I remember a time, about a month after the eldest was born, when he began to make a sound "waa" which was not a crying sound. We, the proud parents, were so excited, "Kosuke spoke!" we exclaimed. Soon he was saying, "ah, ah, ah," in rising and falling tones when he was in a good mood, before sleep, etc.

All babies, one day as if they've suddenly "got it", begin to use their lips to consistently make sounds like "mamama" and "bababa". In reply, the parents say, "Good boy," or "Are you hungry?", etc. When a baby wants something, he says "mamama". Of course he calls food "mamama".

The mother, called "mommy" or "mother" in English, "madre" or "mama" in Spanish, "mei"

in Thai, "omma" in Korean, and "mama" in Chinese, is generally the one who provides milk and food. The fact that all over the world the word for "mother" usually includes the "m" sound may be a legacy of this. It's quite likely that around the world babies follow the same path in the discovery of language.

Our middle child was always teased by his older brother, but one day when he was 2 1/2 he began to fight back, screaming loudly as he attacked. His older brother yelled out an adult expression of the sort used by Japanese mafia types. Something like, "Put up yer dukes and fight like a man. I'll pound ya into the ground, ya rat!" Without thinking, I became angry and yelled, "Who's using such dirty words?" After a moment of quiet consideration, my son answered calmly, "Daddy." I was speechless. Then I murmured to myself, "But Daddy was at his wit's end, too."

Every morning I awake to the monsters. "Mama, I'm hungry! Hurry up and make breakfast," says the eldest. "Mama, hungy," says the middle child. And there's the youngest, tightly grasping the edge of the table, leaning forward on the tips of his toes, and crying "Mama, Mama".

They are all communicating the same message. Language follows a path from the broad outline of the whole down to the details of the parts.

Follow the Natural Path
and You Can't Make a Mistake

Our friends, Matthias and Karin, are Germans who live in the United States. We were really happy when their son, Mark, was born just one month after our second son, Genya.

When Mark was not quite two, my husband went to the United States on business, and visited Matthias' home. Although they live in the U.S., Matthias' family naturally speaks German at home.

My husband was really surprised to find Mark, the same age as Genya, speaking so much. Compared with Mark, Genya's language came late. When Mark was playing with toys, or drawing pictures, he was always chattering – in German, of course. To Mark's fluent chatter, his mother, Karin, and his father, Matthias, would reply, "Ja, ja, wirklich?" (Yeah, yeah, really?).

Because Mark was speaking so much, my husband began to wonder what he was saying, and asked Karin, "What did he just say?" Karin grinned and laughed, answering, "I have no idea!"

To my husband, who speaks a little German, even when he listened closely, Mark's chatter definitely sounded like German. The sounds and the rhythm were clearly German. But German *baby-talk*, it seems.

When I heard that, I was intrigued. Looking from the outside at my Genya, he was saying, "Ga, ga, ga ~ tte, ga, ga ~ tte, ga, ~ ta yo. It doesn't make sense. But how would it sound to someone who spoke only a little Japanese? Probably very much like perfectly complete Japanese.

Mark and Genya have already absorbed the sound patterns of German and Japanese from the repeated conversations of the people around them. They have just one more step to go.

Language which is acquired through a pattern of sounds will be spoken without any thought of mistakes in pronunciation or grammar, because pronunciation and grammar are contained in the patterns. There is no need to worry about mistakes in the process of natural acquisition.

I'll never forget something one of my Korean friends once said to me. "Why do you speak such natural Korean – just like a native speaker? How come you never make any grammar mistakes?" When she said that, I was at a loss, because at that time I was totally ignorant of Korean grammar.

Language Acquired Unconsciously

This story is about when my eldest son, Kosuke, was 3 1/2 years old. One night, around dinner time, the phone rang. Kosuke dashed to answer it and said, "Hello, Hiraoka speaking." [In Japan, this is a common way to answer the phone, giving the family name.] Until then, his style had been more like, "Hello. Who's that? Grandpa, grandma, oooh, Daddy?" My husband and I looked at each other, realizing he had picked up "Hiraoka speaking" without us even noticing it.

Just then, Kosuke turned from the receiver to look over at us with a puzzled expression and said, "Mama, am I Hiraoka?" My husband and I almost fell out of our chairs with surprise.

Another time, we had this conversation. "Mom, I was super-active today, wasn't I?" "Uh-huh." "Super-active means *very* active, right?" "That's right." "What's *active*?"

Was he using the words without understanding their meaning? Perhaps he couldn't write their definition down on a vocabulary list, but he was understanding the *general* meaning. Although constantly acquiring new words, he didn't often ask these kind of questions. Most of the time, he stored up sounds without question which would come forth unconsciously when the appropriate situation arose.

This reminded my adult self of something that happened when I went on a HIPPO homestay to France. My host father was showing me all the fruit trees in his garden, one-by-one, when the

sounds, "C'est pour manger?" sprang from my mouth. My host father replied, "Oui, bien sûr, très bon." (Yes, of course, they're very good.) When I heard that, I said to myself, "Oh, you can eat them."

At that moment, I felt startled. What was it that I had just said? Although I said it myself, I didn't know what I had said. When I said it, I hadn't thought of the meaning I wanted and then decided to say it. It all occurred spontaneously. The sounds of the tape came back to me as I realized it was from the HIPPO tape I always played at home. This was the section where the line, "Is this good to eat?" appeared in French.

This kind of experience is impossible when memorizing language word-by-word – this word means this and it is used at such and such a time. It was that way for me when I took English in school. I was always thinking in my head, "Is this the right word? Is this OK? Am I making a mistake?"

Sounds without meaning, heard repeatedly, are stored inside the body unconsciously, together with situational information. Later, we are able to use expressions we thought we didn't know when they are automatically called forth by the appropriate situation. This is how babies acquire language. Now, the baby in me has been reborn.

Language Develops
in an Open Mind

Parents understand their children.

He hadn't seen grandpa in a while, but immediately my middle son began earnestly telling him, "Eefeater buto, bap, baguys, dat!" Seeing grandpa's puzzled look, my eldest son explained, "Beefighter kabuto went zap and killed the bad guys, just like that!" "TV," I added.

Compared with his older brother, my middle son was very late with language. But early or late – it doesn't matter. I didn't worry about it. Besides, this stage of language acquisition is really interesting.

Often people around him couldn't understand what my middle child was saying. But generally speaking, his father, older brother and I could all understand him. Anyone who spent a lot of time with him, or who was close to him, was able to understand him. There was no need to measure him against some arbitrary standard of language development.

When I went on homestays, exactly the same thing happened. At first, I couldn't understand what my hosts were saying as well as I had expected. But within 2 or 3 days, I was generally able to understand them. And about the same time, they were pretty much able to understand me. I would say to myself, "Wow, I can really communicate well!"

    But then, my hosts' friends would come over, and when they spoke to me, I couldn't understand a thing. However, if my host repeated the same thing, I could understand it perfectly.

    Conversely, when I couldn't communicate what I wanted to say, my host would interpret for me, "This is what she is saying." Listening on the side, I would say to myself, "Yes, yes, that's it exactly." I understood precisely what my host was saying.

    When I heard a Spanish expression just once, it was caught in a Spanish "net" inside of me. As that happened over and over, my language increased. I found many different ways to say the same thing. At first, I could only communicate with my host, but before I knew it, I could also understand and be understood by other friends and families.

    Language is something which grows out of an active interaction and effort toward understanding between people. Little by little, the circle of understanding grows wider.

    Without the interaction of humans, there can be no language. Language is something that is born and nurtured between people.

Baby-Talk is Adults' First Step Too!

Eleven years ago, responding to the HIPPO call, "Here at home in Japan, adults too, can acquire languages naturally like children," I joined the HIPPO Family Club. My husband thought it sounded interesting and encouraged me to go ahead with it, while he continued to hide behind his own wall.

My heart warmed at the thought that together with my 1 1/2 year-old daughter who spoke a smattering of Japanese, I would be acquiring languages of other countries "like a baby." As the sounds of many languages began to resound in our home, I had the sense of having leaped into a free and open new world.

After a year, I could say at least a few words in many different languages. When my daughter was three, one day she suddenly said, "Omma, uyu chuseyo." This means "Mama, milk please," in Korean. I automatically answered, "Yogi itta." (OK, here you are.)

My daughter and I both felt like joyful geniuses. At first, it was like a secret code that only the two of us could understand. But my husband would look at us coldly and say, "That's really pretentious the way you mix other languages in with Japanese, when you can't even speak them well." He couldn't feel my high-flying joy. Besides that, the Korean and Spanish that I spoke with my daughter were not foreign languages – they were our language. On the other hand, the language, besides Japanese, which I supposedly knew the best – the English of my school days – mysteriously would not come out of my mouth. It wasn't until I was able to speak several other languages that, as if I suddenly remembered it, I started to speak English.

Initially my husband was only tolerant of the tapes, which I played constantly as background music and which were just noise to him. Then he began to involuntarily mimic the phrases of my daughter and myself. Little by little his interest deepened, and before we knew it, he could speak several languages.

Now he joins in our multilingual conversations. Unintentionally, almost without realizing it, he went from HIPPO outsider to insider.

When our daughter reached elementary school age, and I casually spoke to her in German or Korean, she would reply, "I don't understand. Say it in Japanese!" One of those times I said, "When you were a baby and I spoke Japanese to you, it wasn't because I thought you understood Japanese. It was because I knew that some day you would be able to understand and speak Japanese. And just as I expected, in no time you were able to speak, weren't you?"

As I said this, I had the feeling I had made a major discovery. But what did my daughter make of all this, and how did it affect her?...

Soon after, Mrs. Kim came from Korea to do a homestay with us. My daughter spoke to her in Korean. I was pleasantly surprised to hear her correctly using a Korean phrase which she had been asking the meaning of just a few days before. As I heard her speaking naturally, Korean came easily to me, too.

Now as sounds fly from my mouth, I begin to see their meaning for the first time. Without realizing it, I have become a "baby."

First Come Sounds
-then Letters

One day when my daughter was in the sixth grade she came home from school smiling happily. She had just begun to learn to read Romaji. [a system for writing Japanese using the Romanized alphabet.]

"Mom, I can read English a little. I'm beginning to understand how to read it. When the sound is "aah" it's written "AR," "ER," or an "R" comes at the end. And when an "S" comes at the end, that means more than one, I guess."

"Where did you see English letters?" I asked. "They're all over town," she said. "There are signs everywhere. I know lots of English sounds and if I read the signs according to the rules of Romaji, but with an English-sounding accent, they turn into English words I know." Using Romaji she guessed the sounds and matched that with the English sounds stored up inside of her.

In natural language acquisition, children encounter writing after they are already able to speak. In fact, when we encounter Japanese writing in school, using guesswork, we sound out the letters and words, matching them with Japanese sounds that we already know.

Now that she was starting to read English, my daughter was following the same path she had taken as a little girl beginning to read Japanese when she recognized the "u" sound of unagi (eel) and udon (noodles) on signs.

When she entered junior high school and received her first English textbook, she said,

"Mom, I can read more and more in my textbook." Her eyes sparkled and she forgot to eat dinner in her excitement.

Since her body was filled with English sounds, she was able to read aloud in beautifully natural English. There was an American who came to teach English conversation in her school several times a month. My daughter wondered, "Why is it that I can understand everything he says?" Through the natural process, first speaking and then writing, my daughter had acquired both spoken and written English.

Surprisingly, during the early days of HIPPO activities, languages such as Korean and Russian were flying around. But, English – the one we're supposed to know the best, because it's the one we all learn in school – went almost unheard. Probably this was the result of all our unpleasant encounters with foreign language learning in school.

At HIPPO, adults and children are on the same level as they discover the natural world of language. Going through this natural process together, the adults finally began to speak English. When we met an English-speaker, instead of lining up the words in our heads, the English came out naturally from our mouths. We didn't wonder whether we were making mistakes.

In this natural process we begin first by speaking a new language. Then once we are speaking, writing too, becomes a precious language treasure.

A Lifetime of Growth from a Single Homestay

"Mom, in Canada, I never heard anyone say 'delicious'. They say 'yum, yum'. But, before eating, they say 'yummy'. 'Yum' and 'yummy' are a little different.

Last summer, my 7th grade daughter, Maya, went on a one-month homestay to Canada. Now, she's always talking about her host family and her life with them. Her way of looking at things is so fresh, I never tire of listening to her. With respect to English, she's also made some unexpected discoveries.

"I thought 'You're welcome' was the proper reply to 'Thank you', but actually there's lots of things you can say. Sometimes you can say 'It's OK' or 'It's nothing' or 'No problem', or even 'Uh-huh'. Each one has a slightly different nuance," said my daughter. As I listened to this, I remembered that I had had the same kind of experiences when we hosted families from all different countries.

My daughter told me that in Canada she had been troubled one day by not knowing how to say in English that she had forgotten her camera. But, when they got into the car, she said, "I don't have my camera," and her host mother replied, "OK, we'll leave for grandma's after you go back in the house and get your camera." Maya then said, "I'm sorry, Mom," and her host mother answered, "It's OK." Maya enjoyed the discovery that even if you don't know a particular word, there's always a different way to say what you want to say.

The number of words we know doesn't seem to be an issue. We can say anything we need to, using just the words we do know. Children are always doing that.

One day after returning from Canada, my daughter yelled in English, "Watch out!," at her little brother who was walking in the road. At first it had an unfamiliar sound, and in spite of myself, I wondered what English word it was. When I asked my daughter, she replied nonchalantly, "It means, 'Be careful'. I knew the first time I heard it."

With other languages besides English, my daughter and I are both involved in natural acquisition, but when it comes to English – against my will – I start thinking about the grammar and spelling of my high school days. I swing back and forth between traditional language learning methods and our HIPPO way of personal discovery. I can't seem to help it.

My daughter's one month homestay is over, but her experiences continue to grow and expand as a result. Talking with friends she made on the trip, there are new discoveries. Listening to the English in the HIPPO tapes we play at home, it seems like she is visualizing the Canadian landscape and hearing the voice of her host mother.

"Canada's not over for me. I'm going back someday," says my daughter. These days we are feeling thankful for the warmth and variety of all the people in our lives.

A Kinder, Gentler Self

After my daughter, Maya, returned from Canada she talked about it every day. Opening her photo album she'd say, "I want to go back to Canada tomorrow."

Since she'd entered junior high school, Maya had begun to talk back to me in an argumentative manner. "This must be adolescence," I thought when we were often angry with each other.

While she was in Canada, it was a very long month for those of us waiting back home. The funny thing was that on her return from the Canadian homestay, Maya seemed kinder and gentler, even to her parents' eyes.

"How did you turn into such a sweet girl?" I asked. "Well, I got a lot of love in Canada. I got lots of love from my host Mom, Dad, my host sister, Joann, and even my brother, Bradley. They really cared about me," she said.

I understood then that she had not been a guest in the Craig family home, but had been a daughter in the family. It seems the Craig's love made Maya appreciate her own family more. She's still our daughter, but now I feel an obligation to her other family in Canada, who helped bring her sweetness back, to continue to bring her up that way.

I used to take being at home with my daughter for granted, but now I'm really happy when

we can be together. As I listen to my daughter's tales of life in Canada, I think there must be parents, too many to count, who have had this same kind of wonderful experience through the HIPPO exchange programs.

Maya said, "My homestay wasn't always perfect. There were times when I wondered what was going on, or when I hated what was happening. But then I would think, 'Well, never mind that! Not everything is perfect in Japan either.' And I came to be able to see things from a variety of viewpoints." 'Never mind' may sound careless, but it's actually quite a mature attitude. My daughter definitely found a new path to wisdom in life.

At HIPPO we often describe natural language acquisition in terms of "From the whole to the parts" or "From general to specific." I'm beginning to think that as we become adults, people become excessively attached to the little things in life, the "parts." And then we lose sight of the big picture. When I have troubles, I try to remember my daughter's positive attitude of "Never mind that."

Meeting many different people and discovering languages through HIPPO, I know I will continue to find many reasons to be glad I was born a human being. We live our lives using language as the key to discovering the world.

I Didn't Know
I Spoke French!

English language education completely ruined my self-confidence. When I joined the HIPPO Family Language Club 15 years ago, it was only because they were offering the Korean language. At that time, HIPPO had just three languages in addition to Japanese – English, Spanish, and Korean. Later, HIPPO had seven languages, and now has eleven languages.

I listened right along to the tapes over the years, but French and English always remained outside my consciousness. Luckily, HIPPO story tapes change language with each change of scene in the story, so there is no way to avoid a particular language. Without consciously listening, I still heard the English and French.

As a HIPPO "old timer", I became known as "Ieru-who-can-speak-eleven-languages," but the truth is that I was never able to speak French. The sounds of French were always a muddle to me.

Last summer, at my husband's insistence, I agreed to go to France on a homestay, but I dreaded the thought of it. For six months, I reluctantly played the French tapes while endlessly saying to myself, "Je ne parle pas français." (I don't speak French.)

We stayed in the beautiful and quiet town of Angers, which was filled with small chateaux and located near the Loire River. We ate breakfast, lunch, and dinner on the outdoor terrace. While the children played with sheep and cats in the big yard, I fully enjoyed the delicious French food and the conversation.

    I was really surprised by my French. Although I had thought I couldn't speak at all, when I was actually compelled to go to France, I had no sense of any language barrier. The French spoken by my host family was very clear and I could understand them easily.

    My son, who was just 1 1/2 at the time, was at that stage where he still couldn't speak, but he could understand everything I said to him. My French and his Japanese were alike in this way. Even when I couldn't answer my hosts with sounds, our conversation flowed with my gestures. There was never a time when I couldn't grasp the overall meaning of what was being said to me. Just like with my son. This was completely different from the experience I had had with English in school, of understanding the words one-by-one, but missing the overall meaning.

    More and more over the course of our stay in France, I began to unconsciously repeat back the French which was spoken to me. "Oh, this is how I should say that," I would think. My hosts' French was steadily passed on to me. In just a short week's time, I was able to speak French with a fair amount of ease. When I heard the sounds of the French language, they resonated with the French sounds from the HIPPO tapes which had been stored up inside of me. As a result, I could understand the basic meaning of the sounds, and I was able to imitate them.

    Language depends on the storing up of a rich variety of sounds, collected from the world around us, inside ourselves. That, always accessible, source helps the sounds to leap suddenly to our lips when we enter a conducive environment.

Each Language Has a Unique Melody

I was born in Marugame City on the island of Shikoku in western Japan. Since my marriage, I've lived in Yokohama (near Tokyo) for six years, and I can speak the "Standard Japanese" of Tokyo, but my first language is Sanuki-ben (the regional Japanese of the Marugame area). People from the Tokyo area lump it all together as Kansai-ben (the Japanese of western Japan), but actually there are major variations from town to town. I can distinguish between the language of Marugame, and of Sakaide or Zentsuji, the towns on either side. When I hear a voice on TV, I can tell for sure if that person happens to be from my hometown.

Whenever I got a call from home, as soon as I knew it was from my mother I automatically switched to Sanuki-ben. It's not just a difference in language – from my gestures to my facial expressions, I became a "Shikoku girl" again. The funny thing is, when my husband says, "Speak Sanuki-ben," I can't. I can't speak it unless I have someone to speak with me.

I have finally come to understand that the experience of a multilingual speaker is not very different from my experience with Sanuki-ben. When the sounds of a conversation partner resonate in harmony with sounds inside us, then we can speak.

As for typical English-language learning in Japan – first we think of the phrase in Japanese, then we marshal the correct grammar and vocabulary, check our pronunciation, OK, no mistakes, let's go! – and out the English phrase stumbles. That's not language. Language is the phenomena which occur in the depths of our consciousness. When adults join with friends to take a fresh approach to a new language, they discover language at the moment that even one phrase leaps naturally from their mouths.

With multilingualism, there's no mixing up of languages. Most people can't differentiate among them the first time they hear eleven languages. It's as if lines of white, red, yellow, and blue chalk are randomly criss-crossed on a blackboard. After several months, anyone can recognize which language they are hearing. Yellow lines gather with the yellow group, red with red.

Language can also be compared to music. Each language has it's own melody, rhythm and harmony – it's own complete music. There's no way to mix two different pieces of music. Our ears can hear even the slight differences in the music of a neighboring town.

Now, when I hear the music of Chinese, I instinctively reply in Chinese – when I hear the music of Spanish, I instinctively reply in Spanish. But, if I stop to think, "Now how do you say that in Spanish?" I lose the ability to speak.

It was the same way when I went on an exchange to France. As long as I listened to the big wave, the entirety, of what someone was saying to me, conversation flowed freely. But, as soon as I got caught up in listening to specific sounds and looking for the meaning of particular words, the flow of meaning would come to a stop and I'd lose my way. I couldn't get back to the original smooth flow.

Wherever we went in France, my 16 month-old son was always speaking any sounds he could imitate, like "le chat" (cat) and "vache" (cow). To questions in French, he replied reflexively "Oui" and "Non." He was never lost.

Adults are Prodigies Too!

The language world we discovered when we adults became "multilingual babies" is completely different from what I had previously imagined. Although I had thought of babies in terms of what they couldn't do yet, actually babies already have just what they need to live well at each level. Once I realized that, I could appreciate the potential of the "baby" inside of me.

As soon as he was finally able to sit up on his own, my son began to spin in time to the music at HIPPO meetings. He didn't do it randomly. Instead, he mimicked the movements of the people around him, going round and round as they moved right or left. Although he couldn't walk yet, I realized he was walking, in his own way. He was expressing with everything he had, "I'm part of the group, too."

And he also was saying, "You adults talk of having learned to sit up, to speak, and to walk, but I've been able to walk and to speak right from the beginning. I've had the potential to fully do these things in me all the time – I didn't have to "learn" anything. At first it seems dangerous to walk without holding on. I crawl, but if I fall I'm OK. And, suddenly one day, I'll stand and walk alone."

Nature has a systematic order to it. Everything proceeds step by step, with no omissions, toward a goal. One day, when my daughter had just begun to walk, she burned herself and started crying and wailing. I pointed to her injured left hand and repeated, "Poor Tomo-chan has

a boo-boo. Let's be careful, OK?" as I comforted her.

A few days later, she fell and hit her head. Pointing to her head and to her left hand, she appealed to me. Although she didn't make a sound, I understood her immediately. "Tomo-chan, boo-boo?" I thought I was seeing the birth of the human "capacity to discover language" right before my eyes. As my son begins to walk and my daughter begins to talk, I can see them expanding their limits more and more.

Let's learn from babies. Here and there "baby field" HIPPO discussion groups are beginning to form. But, observing babies from the outside, we soon get bogged down in "He said this, he said that. She can do this, she can do that. What happened with such and such?" As long as we observe babies from the outside, we lose sight of what they are really about. Likewise, if we observe language from the outside, although we may be able to analyze pronunciation, vocabulary, and grammar, we lose sight of the big picture of the natural language world.

At last, through multilingual activities, adults are able to remember their forgotten experiences as babies. Sharing these experiences we are finally able to see what's happening to babies from the inside.

The natural world of language doesn't differentiate between children and adults, as long as they are humans. Babies are geniuses. Adults are geniuses, too.

No Classes,
No Teachers,
No Test!

"I've got it, I've got it," adults and children exclaim joyfully. This is the scene at HIPPO Family neighborhood clubs. It begins with small discoveries. "Yesterday I couldn't say it, but today I've got it!... I can understand what I'm saying! [when I mimic the tape]... I communicated using Thai!... I don't know how it happened but I can speak!," etc. People's preconceived ideas are shattered as the world opens wide before them. HIPPO creates this kind of brightness and joy.

One day I was surprised by something I saw at Azabujuban Park. There were children of many countries playing there. So, naturally there were many languages flying about. But there was one common language – and it was Japanese. I was surprised to hear completely natural Japanese coming from the mouths of blond-haired, blue-eyed children.

Then I remembered the story of a friend of mine who had been to Boston. In Boston, people gather from all over the world. The park is a melting pot, and all kinds of languages can be heard. Children who play there everyday can speak complete English within six months to a year.

I thought that was completely natural. So, why was I surprised to see the same natural thing happening in a park in Japan?

For these children, their goal was not to be able to speak Japanese or English. They wanted to be able to participate, and so they searched desperately for a common place. While

creating this community place, they acquired language along the way.

In the park, there were no language study corners for "Lesson 1" and "Lesson 2," no curriculum, no division of class according to ability. And of course, there was no teacher, no tests, and no need to worry about mistakes.

There was only the desire to join with favorite friends to build a community. The children did not concern themselves with skin color, or differences between countries.

At HIPPO, we've been searching for an environment which nurtures multilingualism for the past 15 years. Little by little, we're beginning to realize the right environment. It isn't something that we've found, but rather something that we members have created together.

When I moved to Totsuka (in Yokohama, near Tokyo) 6 years ago, there wasn't even one HIPPO club there. For the sake of my family, I decided to start a club. Paralleling the birth of my two children and the growth of my family, new HIPPO clubs have grown up in my neighborhood. The once a week multilingual park has now become a place I can go everyday if I feel like it.

All kinds of people join HIPPO – from babies to senior citizens, without regard to age or country. People who have been active for years and people who have just joined up today are members in equal standing. Three cheers for the adult "babies" playing joyfully in the multilingual park.

Stop Worrying and Just Speak!

It was only 5 days since I had returned from my homestay in Nahodka, and I couldn't wait to share my happiness with my HIPPO friends. As I began to tell them about my experiences - lo and behold - I was speaking in Russian. I wasn't using Russian words that I consciously knew, and I wasn't thinking of what I wanted to say first and then translating to Russian. It was more like "the sounds welled up from inside my body and my mouth worked on its own" as I recalled my many experiences with Ira. Without thinking about it, I was able to communicate whatever I wanted to say.

Since joining HIPPO, I've listened to a lot of languages on tape, and met people of many cultures. I didn't acquire even one of these languages by reading and writing, or by studying grammar, or by being taught by someone else. I used to think this process of self discovery alone was the "natural acquisition of language", but I was missing something important.

As I imitated the sounds on the tapes, and gradually was able to pronounce the sounds of Spanish or French, I listened intently to the tapes in order to discover the meaning in Japanese or English as soon as possible. The moment when meaning attaches to a previously meaningless sound is very joyful. As these experiences multiplied, I began to feel I could speak the languages. The joy of this made me even more enthusiastic about listening to the tapes.

However, when the new Russian tapes came out, I made a resolution to try more thoroughly to have the experience of a baby. That was as a result of my realization that when a baby discovers language, the baby has no other language with which to compare and substitute. I

decided to try my best to keep everything loose, to listen to the sounds without worrying too much about meaning, and to concentrate on having fun with my HIPPO friends.

In Nahodka, I intensely felt the kindness of the people there. Later, when my image of Nahodka became a spring of words bubbling over, I felt as if I had uncovered the secret of how babies acquire language easily. It was as if sounds stored inside me while I was unaware were called forth by the scene. When those sounds resulted in communication, that was their "meaning". Having come to adulthood through "standard foreign language education", I had mistakenly thought that "meaning" was something found in a dictionary. Now, I think dictionary meaning is a kind of secondary meaning.

Within 3 years from my first exposure to Russian, I was able to talk about HIPPO activities and homestay programs with the Nadhoka Superintendent of Education and discuss complicated matters with a customs official at the airport. During that time, I never once tried hard to "find out the meaning" of any Russian words. I laughed with my HIPPO friends, "It sounds like isshobin (a big bottle of sake)!" I became a member of the Russian family who called me Rita and gave me their love. I felt happy and comfortable together with them. And in no time, hardly noticing how it had happened, I was able to speak Russian. This is the way of babies. Upon discovering this "baby-like" self of mine, I found that other languages too had become easy and natural to me. This was true "natural acquisition".

A Bigger World with New Friends

It's hard to believe, but it's been 15 years since I first joined the HIPPO Family Club. Normally, I'm the kind of person who loses interest in things quickly. In addition, I'm single and live alone, so I don't have anyone at home to encourage me to keep it up. The reason why I've continued with HIPPO is because of the people involved.

Just as I have my Russian family, now in Taiwan, Mexico and Thailand, there are people who are very important to me. I treasure the languages which bring those faces to me. But, it is not only across the sea in faraway places that I have important people and languages. On an everyday basis, I value the friendships which brought me into HIPPO.

One day at HIPPO, a five year-old boy yelled, "I want to do Shonben!" (Shonben means "pee-pee" in Japanese.) "Shonben? Do you need to go to the bathroom?" someone asked. "No, the Shonben Song!" The adults looked puzzled. What song was this? Then his mother said, "I know. He means 'Shortening Bread'." That's an English-Language song on the HIPPO tapes.

It's true, with Japanese pronunciation, we're not singing "Shortening Bread." Actually, Shonben sounds much closer. Ever since then, all we can hear is Shonben. The adults are always laughing, as we loudly sing Shonben.

Another day, one of the mothers said laughingly, "On the Chinese tape, there's a phrase which sounds like Yozora" ("night sky" in Japanese). A few days later, a different mother told us, "Mr. Lee from Taiwan came to visit us. Afterwards we drove him home, and as we were about to

part he said, "Yozora" (Oh, you're leaving now). She reported excitedly, "When I thought 'Oh he's used the phrase we were talking about the other day' and 'It's used in this context' I felt really happy, despite my sadness at saying goodbye.

Sometime later, another mother remarked, "When I went to Taiwan on a homestay, I noticed that the children said, 'Zo, zo' (Let's go) when they went out to play. I suddenly realized that this 'Zo' must be the same as the 'Zo' in 'Yozora'."

"When I hear 'Yozora', I don't know why, but I answer with the sound, 'Topaochun' (Take care)," continued one father. In this way, the dialogue continued to grow.

This kind of discussion - "That's like such and such in Japanese"- may not seem to have a direct relationship to language acquisition. But actually this is the hidden secret to human, instinctive discovery and development of language. Humans depend on impressions of all scenes and sounds in order to take in language.

Even when it's a phrase I already know, it's reborn as something new in my friend's discovery of it. It becomes the special language which brings my friend to mind.

Discovering new worlds within the context of human relations is the basic meaning of "natural language acquisition." Therefore, no matter how well or how many languages we speak, there is no graduation from HIPPO.

Mathematics is a Language

At HIPPO, there is a college called Transnational College of LEX, Torakare or TCL for short. This college has no tests, no grades, no class divisions by grade level or ability, and no boundaries between liberal arts and the sciences. It is the "world's smallest college." The students are of all kinds, from recent high school graduates to grandmothers. They all use HIPPO activities as a base from which they consider human language to be a natural phenomenon, and research this phenomenon from various approaches according to a natural science methodology.

I enjoyed HIPPO activities very much, so when I graduated from college I became a student of TCL. However, it happened that my greatest nemesis in the world was mathematics. In high school, I was continually having to take make-up tests. Because I couldn't understand it, I hated math; because I hated it, I never tried; because I never tried, I couldn't do it... It was a vicious cycle.

At TCL where the "natural science of human language" is primary, most of the lectures are in "science" fields. But, luckily there are no tests or evaluations, and there is a lot of interesting field work to do, so I didn't have any problems.

Some time after I joined, in order to further the investigation of the scientific side of language - voice analysis - the group began to wrestle with the math of Fourier analysis. At first, my math-phobic self decided that Fourier had nothing to do with me. It was the sounds of my friends' voices, filled with enjoyment, which caused me to make up my mind to take my first

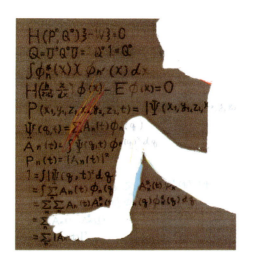

steps forward. Discussions about Fourier mathematics took place everywhere, on the street… at night in a Chinese restaurant. The upbeat mood was like gossiping about a popular soap opera. It was this "you-can-have-fun-talking-about-mathematics" atmosphere that made me decide to challenge Fourier mathematics.

Knowing nothing, all I could do was just dive right in with the rest of the group, cheering all the way. Reading books together with friends and discussing them was a lot of fun. After a few months, at a point where I had no idea how much I understood and how much I didn't understand, I was given a chance to talk to the group in my own way about Fourier.

I gave it all I could. As I was about to speak, I turned to my listeners and the language of Fourier math poured straight from my mouth. It seemed like no time at all, but I talked for 5 hours straight! The feeling I had was completely different from that of simply presenting the things I understood. I felt exactly as if I was creating Fourier mathematics myself. When I was finished, everyone else was as affected as I was. In my heart, I felt that math, which I had so disliked, was actually a beautiful and concise language created by humans to describe nature.

The roots of my "baby-like" experience with the Russian language lie in my experience with mathematics and "The Fourier Adventure." Since Fourier, my attitude with regard to languages and humans has changed completely. I have stopped trying to use shortcuts to get where I'm going, and now I truly believe that languages are given to us by the people around us.

Natural Science: Researching the Obvious

A thick layer of butter spread over rye bread and topped with ikura (salmon roe). Until recently, that was my daily view of the table in Russia. Just like in Japanese, the word in Russian for salmon roe is "ikura." Initially I was surprised, but the Japanese word has its roots in Russian.

When I first started listening to the Korean tapes, I realized how many words there are which sound just like Japanese. Moreover, my closed attitude "Japanese is Japanese" began to break open as I found many times that Japanese sounds were related to Korean. For example, "tari" means legs in Korean. It is pronounced "ashi" in Japanese when it means legs, but as "tari" in the compound "tarinai" (lacking, not enough). Another example was "noppo." This means tall in Korean, and in Japanese "seitaka noppo" means tall and lanky. It's obvious that "tari" and "noppo" originated in Korea, proving the fact that languages of neighboring countries influence each other. Even today, the Japanese language is changing every day. The more I hear of examples such as the Japanese word "saboru" (to neglect [one's duty] or to play hooky) which actually comes from the French "sabotcur", the less strange they seem to me.

Through these discoveries, we at TCL quickly became interested in going back to the time period of the root language of Japanese, Yamato. Putting our hands on the oldest Japanese literature - Kojiki, Nihonshoki, and Manyoshu - we were again surprised by something which is generally taken for granted. They were written entirely in kanji. Kanji are Chinese characters. [Modern Japanese is written with a combination of kanji, and hiragana and katakana, which are indigenous Japanese syllabary.] Are we to believe that Chinese characters crossed the sea all on their own? Actually many people and a lot of culture came along with language from China and the Korean peninsula.

Like today, in the time of Yamato there were various languages and cultures which influ-

enced each other. If we assume the presence of Korean and Chinese language, and avoid compartmentalizing everything into the ancient Japanese language of Yamato, the lively language of the authors Kakinomotono Hitomaro and Nukatanookimi [who wrote the above classics] is easily seen. Reinterpreting the words left behind by these authors in a multilingual context, the centuries between now and then evaporate, and we get a vivid view of ever-constant human beings. This view is imparted in our books, "The Code of Hitomaro" and "The Code of Nukatanookimi."

Before we knew it, these ancient authors had become our good friends. They gave us the message that the Japanese language is not a discrete "thing", it is constantly being recreated through the interaction of people. In my experience, math is the same. Neither exists outside of humans. They are born from humans and continually evolving.

Why is it that society came to look upon language - whether Japanese, math, or other languages - as a contrivance outside of humans and nature? These languages have become the main targets of research and debate on how one can most effectively master them.

Rather, at HIPPO we say that language is something which is discovered or created between people. Given the physical ability, children are able to acquire any language. That's because they discover language together with the people around them - and together they build their own language world.

Through participation in HIPPO activities I've come to realize a simple fact which, although profound, is rarely noted. The ability to speak (acquire) languages naturally is what makes us human and a part of nature. To describe the nature of languages and how humans can acquire them so naturally is the goal of the natural science of language.

Ears, Mouth and Heart are Open to any Language

Just by accident, I became good friends with a young man from Kenya named John. He spoke English beautifully. When I asked him, "How many languages do you speak?" he answered, "Six – English, German, French, Spanish, Italian, and a little Japanese."

When I asked, "What about African languages?" John seemed surprised, but after thinking a bit, he replied, "I can only speak about 15." "Only 15." I was amazed. When I asked, he explained that in his multilingual country they have Swahili as a common language, plus English, plus over 100 indigenous languages. All these languages are constantly flying about. As far as African languages go, there are many people who can speak more than 15. So, according to John, it's not, "Wow, 15 languages!", but "Only 15 languages." People who live in that kind of environment naturally speak more than one language, and they are very open to new ones.

When I first met John, he had only been in Japan two weeks. So, naturally he knew almost no Japanese. But, as we spoke in English, he would suddenly insert surprisingly natural sounding Japanese phrases into the conversation like "Chotto mattetene." (Wait a moment.) Although he didn't know many words, the ones he used like "Ettone" (Well...) and "~nandayo" (... you see) were the type that you hear over and over, and which sound particularly "Japanese." They seemed as if they had been lifted straight from a Japanese melody. Even when he spoke just one phrase of Japanese, it sounded very natural. During John's three month stay in Japan, he

quickly acquired the ability to speak Japanese, right before my eyes.

"If you think about it, living in a country like Kenya with over 100 languages used on a daily basis, you never know when you're going to encounter a new language. In order to live, whenever you meet a new language you must open your ears to that new language and try to imagine what's being said. Usually you can make a rough guess, no matter what language. That's the beginning. From there, as you become closer to the other speaker, you are able to understand each other, and to speak," says John.

For John, when he first encountered Japanese it was just like any other new language he might meet in Africa. To a real multilingual person, the number of languages is not the issue. I realized that real multilingualism requires a heart which is open to any language and any speaker.

At one time, I'm sure everyone was multilingual. Almost all of the indigenous African languages have no writing systems. Speakers have always depended only on their mouths and ears. But in other parts of the world, with the invention of writing and of the concept of "foreign" languages, people began to close their ears and their hearts to unfamiliar languages.

To John, all languages are human languages, not foreign languages. He is like a baby in that respect. I miss John's smiling face.

There's No Such Thing as a "Foreign" Language at HIPPO

The other day, I heard an interesting story from a Japanese friend I hadn't seen in a long time. My friend's husband was American, and they had lived in New York for a number of years after marrying. During that time, they had a baby. Because they were living in the U.S. and because the father was American, it was natural for them to conduct their lives in English.

They returned to Japan when their baby was 15 months old, at the time when he could understand everything his parents said to him, and he was speaking a few English words like "Mommy" and "Dada".

They moved in with my friend's parents and suddenly everything changed. They were in Grandma and Grandpa's Japanese-speaking world, and, of course, most of the child's new friends were Japanese. A few months passed, and he suddenly began to really speak, but the surprising thing was that most of it was not English. It was age-appropriate complete Japanese.

If you think about this, it's very mysterious. That child was born and brought up in an English-language environment, where he was constantly awash in a shower of English. Naturally his body became filled with English sounds. Then suddenly, his environment became a Japanese-speaking one.

Let's assume that he had to start over from the beginning with Japanese, storing up the sounds as he had with English. Even if we don't allow as much time as he took with English, a

considerable amount would still be required.

But in fact that's not what happened. In just a few short months, he was able to speak Japanese.

This reality tells us that observing language only from the outside, and simply deciding English and Japanese are different is a nonsensical approach. It's true that for every language there are superficial variations in pronunciation and grammar. But, as shown by the previous example of the baby who came from the U.S., all languages have an underlying universal structure created by humans.

To put it boldly, I would like to say that the everyday music of any particular language is just one superficial variation on universal human language. Acquiring the ability to speak any one language means the acquisition of underlying universal human language. Any human who can speak one language will be able to discover and speak other languages if they follow the path of natural acquisition, with universal human language as the foundation.

Let's discover the "sameness" in all humans. It's due to this sameness that we can appreciate the unlimited richness of variety amongst humans. Somewhere along the way, the words foreign language and foreigner have disappeared from HIPPO.

Search for the Baby Within

In the previous 26 articles, members have reported their real-life experiences and adventures with HIPPO Family Club activities. You have probably already noticed our main point, which recurs throughout the articles like a musical theme.

Any human with the physical capability will be able to speak the language of the environment he was born into and brought up in. In fact, this may be the definition of what it means to be "human." I have the feeling that because this fact was a too obvious piece of reality, we had forgotten to wonder "why" it was so. It also seems that adults have forgotten how – if, for example they are Japanese – they acquired Japanese language. We've hidden these memories far away and don't even see the value of rediscovering them.

"Let's build a multilingual world. Adults can become babies too!" That call sounded really pleasant and inviting. But once many languages began to fly about, the adults were lost. Becoming a baby is a great idea, but how are adults supposed to do it?

We began "looking for baby." At the start, we were thoroughly lost, but now it seems as if the "baby" was alive inside of each of us all along. Adults were viewing language from the outside as an inanimate thing, analyzing, dividing it up into the "parts" of pronunciation and vocabulary, then applying these parts according to the "blueprint" of grammar. That's the type of language education found in school.

In contrast, a baby is ensconced in a world of language. He starts from the inside, as a

member of this world, with a broad, general understanding. Gradually, his understanding becomes clearer and more specific as he discovers language and the world. The baby's approach from the inside is the complete opposite of the adult's approach from the outside.

Even when this is understood, it's not so easy for an adult to immediately become a baby. Like riding a seesaw, we tilt back and forth between adults (from the outside) and babies (from the inside). Over time we come closer to babies. Adults begin to experience the same process as babies. Adults, like babies, are humans.

Humans and the language instinctively created by those humans, can only be natural. The goal of natural science is to objectively observe natural phenomena from the outside and find language to describe the hidden underlying order. Until now the science of language could not escape this precedent.

But, we humans have language within us. Through mutual experiences and discussion, we can confirm the universal order of language, from the inside. Describing nature from inside nature leads to the birth of a new natural science.

Until recently, the scene outside the window was pitch-black, but the sky begins to lighten, light quickly breaks, and the dawn is bright with the fresh glow of spring. "Language is light!" I thought for a moment. And, I wondered what world my sons will discover through the light of language.

What's the Transnational College of LEX?
A College Researching "Language and Man" through natural science

In 1983, the Hippo Family Club established the Transnational College of LEX (Torakare) to research the theme "Languages and Man."
Studying patterns of sounds within languages, discovering new interpretations to ancient texts and observing the process of natural language acquisition by babies are just some of the topics covered by the Torakare as it looks at "Languages" as a natural phenomenon of humans. The basis of study lies in the experiences of Hippo Family Club members. There are no grades, no tests, and no curriculums here. Students of various educational backgrounds of the college gather, leading to many wonderful results.